FARTING FARM ANIMALS

COLORING BOOK

Just so stinking cute!

Blow off some steam, and a few farts after a long stressful day by coloring adorable farting farm animals and laugh along with their animal friends.

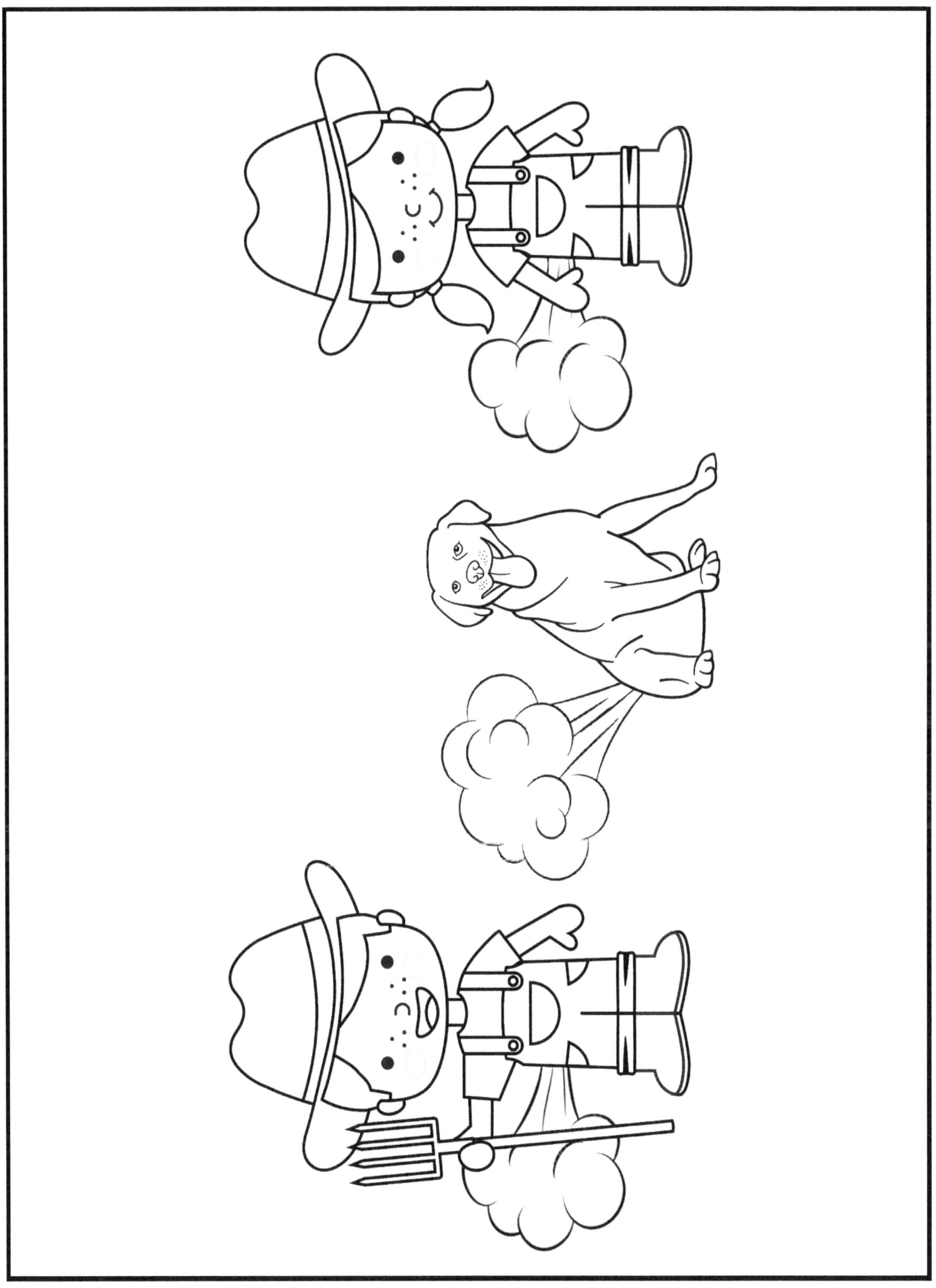

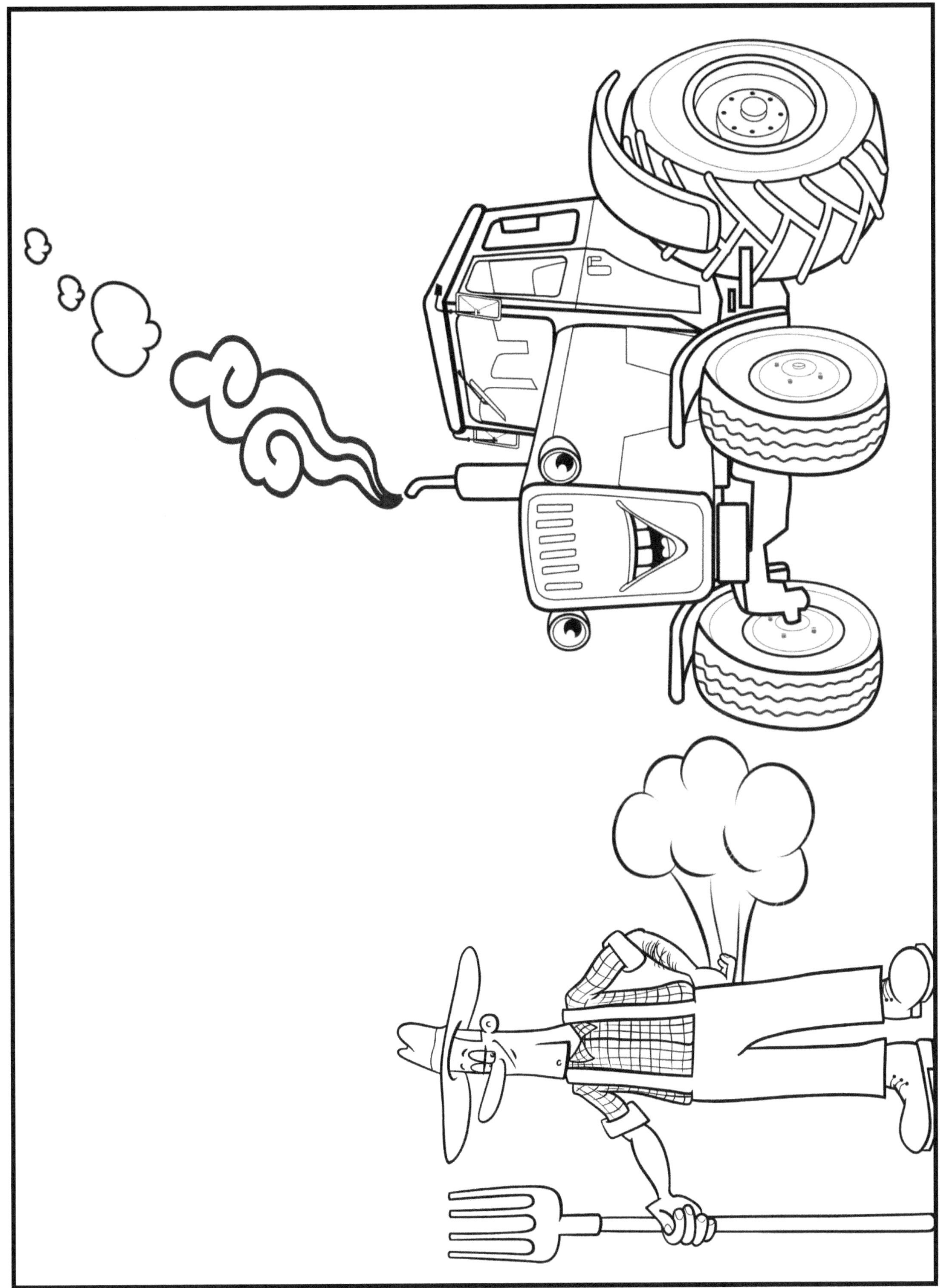

www.ingramcontent.com/pod-product-compliance
Lightning Source LLC
Chambersburg PA
CBHW081233250726
48654CB00012B/1312